Original title:
Weaving Worries into Wishes

Author: Jaxon Kingsley
ISBN HARDBACK: 978-9916-90-170-0
ISBN PAPERBACK: 978-9916-90-171-7

Flickering Flame of Faith

In shadows deep, a flame does dance,
A flicker bright, in nature's chance.
Through storms that rage, it holds its ground,
A beacon warm, where hope is found.

With every doubt, the flame grows strong,
It whispers soft, a sacred song.
In darkest nights, the light will stay,
Guiding hearts along the way.

The Interlace of Emotions

Threads of joy, woven with pain,
In the fabric of life, such is the gain.
Colors clash and blend so bright,
Creating a tapestry of the night.

Laughter echoes, sorrow spills,
In each heartbeat, a world fulfills.
Weaving moments, tender and bold,
Emotions rich, like stories told.

Vibrant Tapestries of Tomorrow

Tomorrow waits, with arms outspread,
A canvas blank, where dreams are fed.
Colors vivid, visions clear,
Building paths with each new year.

With hope as thread and love the loom,
We stitch our fate, dispel the gloom.
In vibrant hues, the future sings,
As every heart takes flight on wings.

Echoes Woven in Time

In the quiet, echoes ring loud,
Whispers of stories, lost in the crowd.
Time weaves its path, a constant flow,
Remnants of moments, we come to know.

In every heartbeat, a tale resides,
Echoes of laughter, where sorrow hides.
Woven in whispers, the past will chime,
Binding our souls, through the march of time.

Hopes Entwined with Fears

In twilight's grasp, dreams softly weave,
Yet shadows whisper what we grieve.
Hope's glinting spark, a fragile thread,
While fear looms close, its heavy dread.

Through tangled paths our hearts will tread,
With every step, our doubts are fed.
Still light breaks forth, a guiding beam,
In the heart's shadow, we find our dream.

The Fabric of Reflection

In the mirror's gaze, stories unfold,
Each wrinkle a tale, each sigh retold.
Threads of the past, stitched with grace,
In silence we wear time's embrace.

Colors fade, yet wisdom thrives,
Patterns remind us how love survives.
Through the fabric, our essence gleams,
Woven in dreams, in life's soft seams.

Comfort in the Threadbare

Nestled in corners where shadows reign,
Old chairs hold whispers of laughter and pain.
Threadbare blankets, memories cling,
Wrapped in warmth, old sorrows sing.

With every tear, a story shared,
In cozy nooks, hearts are bared.
Beyond the fray, still we find grace,
In fragile moments, a warm embrace.

Muted Tones of Transformation

In soft hues, life begins to change,
Fading echoes, a world rearranged.
Whispers of growth in quiet tones,
Through shifting shades, our spirit roams.

Each step forward, a phase laid bare,
As colors blend, we shed our care.
In the stillness, we understand,
These muted tones shape life's grand plan.

The Stitch of Potential

In shadows where dreams quietly dwell,
A thread of hope begins to swell.
With every stitch, a journey's spun,
Potential blooms, like morning sun.

Each fiber woven, strong yet light,
Guiding hearts through darkest night.
A tapestry of wishes and fears,
Crafting futures from silent tears.

Interlaced Aspirations

A dance of threads, colors collide,
In the fabric of dreams, we confide.
Each aspiration a stitch in time,
Creating patterns, rhythm, and rhyme.

Weaving tightly, through joy and doubt,
Interlaced stories, woven out.
Stronger together, we rise and embrace,
The beauty of dreams, time won't erase.

The Warp of Resilience

Amidst the chaos, fibers bend,
Strength in the weave, to never end.
Both fragile and bold, like a river's flow,
In the warp of resilience, we grow.

Tales of struggle, patterns so vast,
Each challenge met, shadows they cast.
Yet through the darkness, light gleams bright,
In resilience, we find our might.

Tangle of Thoughts

In a maze of ideas, we twist and turn,
A tangle of thoughts, for which we yearn.
Threads of confusion, colors entwined,
Within the chaos, peace we find.

Piecing together the shards of our mind,
Creating a mosaic, uniquely defined.
A journey within, to unravel the knot,
In this tangle of thoughts, we discover our lot.

Knots of Knowledge

In the web of stories spun,
Wisdom's threads weave and run.
Each knot a lesson tight and clear,
Binding the heart, calming the fear.

Through trials faced and bridges burned,
In quiet moments, much we've learned.
With every twist, a tale we share,
A tapestry rich, beyond compare.

A Quilt of Resilience

Stitches pulled through thick and thin,
Crafting strength from deep within.
Each patch tells of battles fought,
In every corner, hope is caught.

Layered warmth against the cold,
Stories of the brave and bold.
Together sewn, we find our place,
United threads in life's embrace.

Frayed Edges and New Beginnings

Threads unravel, but do not break,
In frayed edges, a chance to wake.
Life's fabric worn, yet still it gleams,
Promises whispered through our dreams.

From tattered pasts, new paths arise,
Every ending sparks the skies.
With gentle hands, we mend and sew,
Creating futures from what we know.

Whispers Between the Threads

Soft murmurs in the woven space,
Voices of those who leave a trace.
Conversations held in silent art,
Every stitch a beating heart.

In the quiet, secrets bloom,
Fragments of life in every room.
Threads connect what once was lost,
In love's embrace, we count the cost.

Dreams Embroidered in Reality

In twilight's glow, dreams softly weave,
A tapestry formed by those who believe.
Threads of hope in a world so vast,
Stitched with courage, a future cast.

Woven whispers in the gentle night,
Every stitch silently takes flight.
Bound by visions, vibrant and grand,
Each yearning heart lends a guiding hand.

Joy Stitched through Trials

In the midst of storms, we find our way,
Through trials faced, we learn to play.
Stitching joy in fabric of strife,
Embracing the colors that enrich our life.

With every tear, a lesson sewn,
In darkness, a seed of hope is grown.
Together we stand, hearts intertwined,
Finding the light that fate has designed.

Spinning Gold from Gloom

From shadows deep, we spin our gold,
Crafting stories that need to be told.
Winds of change, they bend and sway,
Transforming our fears into bright array.

In every challenge, a shimmer shines,
Dancing through darkness, our spirit aligns.
Through tangled paths, our courage calls,
In the quiet moments, we stand tall.

Colorful Contrasts of the Mind

In hues of thought, we blend and clash,
Vivid dreams in a vibrant splash.
Every shade, a tale to narrate,
In the heart's canvas, we cultivate.

Light and shadow dance and play,
Creating a chorus in shades of gray.
Embrace the contrasts, the highs and the lows,
For in each moment, our richness grows.

Fabric of Tomorrow

Threads of hope in twilight spun,
Dreams are woven, one by one.
Patterns bright, a future's call,
In this tapestry, we stand tall.

Stitches firm, the seams align,
In every heart, the stars do shine.
A canvas painted with our care,
Each moment's thread, a bond we share.

Spools of Solitude and Serenity

In quiet corners, whispers bloom,
Spools of thought in velvet room.
Threads unwind, a gentle flow,
In solitude, the spirit grows.

Softly wrapped in peace's embrace,
Time suspends in a sacred space.
Each thread a story, softly spun,
In silent hours, we are one.

Interlacing Joy with Sorrow

Colors clash in life's grand quilt,
Threads of joy with sorrow built.
Each stitch a lesson, harsh or sweet,
Emotions woven, bittersweet.

From shadows deep to sunshine's grace,
The fabric shifts, a new embrace.
In every tear, a laugh will rise,
In every loss, a new surprise.

The Needle's Pathway

A needle glides through fabric fine,
Tracing paths where dreams entwine.
With every pull, a story's told,
In the weave, our lives unfold.

Gentle hands with purpose guide,
Through twists and turns, we do not hide.
The thread we choose, the life we make,
In the needle's path, our hearts awake.

Mosaic of Longings

In shadows where dreams softly play,
Fragments of hope weave night and day.
Whispers of wishes dance in the air,
Each piece a story, a truth laid bare.

Colors collide in a vibrant display,
Memories linger, refusing to stray.
Yearnings entwine like threads of a seam,
Creating a tapestry, life's gentle dream.

The Weft of Whimsy

A flicker of laughter, a glimmer of light,
Crafting a world where shadows take flight.
Doodles of fancy float through the mind,
In this realm of wonder, delight's intertwined.

With each playful twist, the fabric unfolds,
Stitching together the tales yet untold.
From the chaos arises a dance of the free,
In the weft of whimsy, we find the key.

Twisting Fears into Fantasies

Beneath the surface, anxieties creep,
Yet within the heart, wild visions leap.
Transforming the dark into hues of gold,
Embracing the stories that fear has sold.

A canvas of courage, brave colors ignite,
Crafting illusions that shimmer so bright.
With every shadow turned into light,
We dance through the chaos, hearts taking flight.

Fabricating Futures

Threads of tomorrow weave through today,
Building our hopes in a delicate way.
Dreams are the fabric, resilient and bold,
Creating a future where stories unfold.

With each tiny stitch, intentions align,
A tapestry forming, intricately fine.
Together we rise, forging paths anew,
In the fabric of futures, our spirits break through.

Unseen Threads of Connection

In shadows soft, we find our way,
Invisible ties weave night into day.
Hearts beat in rhythm, though far apart,
Silent whispers echo in every heart.

A glance exchanged, a smile so bright,
Bridges built in the absence of sight.
Through tangled paths and winding roads,
Connections flourish, as love explodes.

Threads that Bind and Break

Tightly woven, these strands we share,
Yet fragile whispers linger in the air.
Moments cherished, but shadows loom,
What once was light can spiral to gloom.

Promises made, but fears can creep,
Threads of trust, they fray and weep.
In silence we stand, unsure and frail,
The ties that bind can also impale.

Woven Whispers of Hope

In the tapestry of dreams, we find,
Threads of hope that intertwine.
Each whisper carries tales untold,
A story of warmth in the winter's cold.

Through storms we rise, our spirits soar,
Each stitch a promise, forevermore.
In darkest nights, the threads will gleam,
Woven together, we weave a dream.

The Symphony of Strands

Each thread a note in grand design,
A symphony of hopes, yours and mine.
Together we dance through life's sweet frame,
In harmony's grasp, we're never the same.

The rhythm of life plays soft and low,
In woven patterns, our spirits grow.
With every heartbeat, a new refrain,
A tapestry crafted from joy and pain.

Threads of Tomorrow

We weave the fabric of today,
Each moment forms a thread,
With colors bright and bold,
We stitch our dreams ahead.

In shadows cast by doubt,
We find the light to shine,
With every step we take,
We craft a grand design.

The future calls our names,
As stars begin to gleam,
With courage, we embrace,
The tapestry of dream.

Threads of Hope

In whispers of the night,
Hope gently weaves its tale,
Through storms and through the strife,
It sings, we shall prevail.

With every tear that falls,
A seed of strength is sown,
For in the heart of pain,
The light of hope is grown.

Together hand in hand,
We journey through the dark,
With every step we take,
We ignite a tiny spark.

Tapestry of Dreams

In twilight's gentle glow,
Dreams dance upon the air,
With threads of silver light,
We weave a world so rare.

Each hope a shining star,
Each wish a vibrant hue,
Together they create,
A canvas, bright and true.

With every heartbeat known,
New patterns start to rise,
A tapestry unfolds,
Beneath the endless skies.

From Fears to Fantasies

We stand upon the edge,
Of doubt and light's embrace,
With every fear faced down,
New dreams we will trace.

In shadows of the mind,
Where worries intertwine,
We break the chains of doubt,
And let our spirits shine.

From whispers to the roar,
Our fantasies take flight,
As we transform our fears,
Into a world of light.

Dreamcatcher of Intentions

In the night sky, stars gleam bright,
Whispers of dreams take their flight.
Threads of hope weave through the air,
Catching wishes, everywhere.

With every sigh, a vision forms,
Anchored in heart, where love warms.
Fleeting thoughts in the gentle breeze,
Wrapped in light, they dance with ease.

Glistening beads, the past flows by,
Dreamcatcher spins, a lullaby.
Intentions set in moonlit glow,
Guiding paths that we shall go.

From dawn till dusk, we chase the light,
In the weave, all feels just right.
Holding close what we believe,
In this tapestry, we achieve.

The Fiber of Belief

Threads entwined in a vibrant hue,
Each a story, old and new.
Woven tight with care and grace,
In the heart, they'll find a place.

Every strand has a tale to tell,
Of rising high and how we fell.
Strength and hope in every twist,
In the fabric of dreams, we exist.

Colors blend in a beautiful way,
For every night there's a hopeful day.
Fingers dance on the loom of fate,
Creating a future we cultivate.

As we stitch, our worries cease,
In the tapestry, we find peace.
Belief the thread that holds us tight,
Guiding us toward the light.

Looming Possibilities

In the shadows, futures gleam,
The loom spins out a vivid dream.
Every choice, a thread so fine,
Weaving paths that intertwine.

Beneath the surface, whispers grow,
Each moment holds a tale to show.
With open hearts, we grasp the chance,
Inviting change into our dance.

The loom supports a vibrant view,
Of what can be and what is true.
Colors swirl with a gentle grace,
In every pattern, we find our place.

So reach for dreams, let go of doubt,
In possibilities, we shout.
The fabric bright, our stories blend,
A tapestry that does not end.

Unraveled Hopes

Once tightly wound, now comes undone,
A tangled web beneath the sun.
Threads of hope begin to fray,
Yet still they glow, they find their way.

In the chaos, beauty lies,
Each thread carries unspoken sighs.
Loose ends dance in the gentle breeze,
Finding freedom, learning to please.

Unraveled dreams can still take flight,
Shimmering softly in the night.
What seems lost can be reclaimed,
As we embrace the wild, untamed.

With courage sewn in every seam,
We gather strength, we dream the dream.
For in the fray, new paths emerge,
Unraveled hopes begin to surge.

Breathe Life into the Loom

Threads of gold, intertwine,
In the fabric, stories shine.
With each weave, a tale to tell,
In the heart, dreams swell.

Colors bright, a canvas vast,
Moments cherished, shadows cast.
Stitch by stitch, hope takes flight,
In the loom, we craft our light.

Gentle hands, so skilled, so true,
Transforming visions, old and new.
With every loop, we find our place,
In the tapestry of time and space.

Breathe in deep, let spirits soar,
In this craft, we find our core.
Life's a dance, we guide the thread,
Together, onward, we are led.

Unfolding Dreams at Dusk

Whispers soft, the evening calls,
As twilight wraps the world in thralls.
In the hush, dreams start to rise,
Painting visions across the skies.

Stars awaken, one by one,
Guiding wishes, the day is done.
In the silence, hope takes root,
In the heart, passions commute.

With each breath, the night unfolds,
Secrets held, and tales retold.
In the shadows, visions gleam,
As we wander through the dream.

Holding tightly, dreams untamed,\nIn the dusk, our spirits
flamed.
Together, let the journey start,
Unfolding dreams within the heart.

The Richness of Resilience

In the storm, we find our strength,
Weathered trials, they go to length.
With each bruise, we learn to stand,
And rise anew, a steady hand.

Through the shadows, we walk tall,
Embracing courage, answering the call.
With every stumble, roots grow deep,
In resilience, our spirits leap.

Richness blooms from broken ground,
In the silence, life's truths are found.
As we gather, hope like gold,
In our hearts, the brave and bold.

So we stand, through thick and thin,
In unity, we rise and spin.
With each heartbeat, we find our way,
In resilience, we choose to stay.

Crafting Tomorrow from Today

In the moment, we hold the key,
To shape the path that we can see.
With each choice, our future grows,
In the heart, potential flows.

Brush in hand, we paint the hour,
With vibrant dreams, we build the power.
In the present, seeds are sown,
Crafting tomorrows, our own throne.

Moments fleeting, yet filled with zest,
In every heartbeat, we invest.
With vision clear, we forge ahead,
Creating life from words unsaid.

So let us dance, let spirits play,
As we craft our dreams today.
In the tapestry of time and fate,
Crafting tomorrow, we celebrate.

The Art of Turning Tears into Triumphs

In sadness we sow the seeds,
From pain, a strength that breeds.
Each tear a drop of grace,
A path to find our place.

With every sorrow, we learn,
From darkness, a light will burn.
In whispers of hope, we rise,
Transforming loss into the prize.

Through trials, we craft our song,
In the heart where we belong.
Each challenge, a chance to grow,
From tears, our triumphs flow.

Patchwork of Possibilities

A quilt of dreams, stitched tight,
Colors blending, bold and bright.
Each piece tells a story true,
In every square, a glimpse of you.

With needle's dance, we weave our fate,
In patterns rare, we elevate.
The threads of hope, they intertwine,
Creating worlds where we can shine.

In patches worn, the love we find,
Embracing change, unconfined.
Through seams of joy and threads of tears,
A tapestry of endless years.

Shadows Lifting to Sunlight

The shadows stretch, then fade away,
As dawn announces a brand new day.
With golden rays, they softly chase,
The darkness that once held our space.

In gentle whispers, sunlight calls,
Breaking through the heavy walls.
Each beam a promise, pure and bright,
Guiding us to take flight.

From hidden fears, we now emerge,
To dance in light, our hearts converge.
In every shadow, lessons gleaned,
Into the warmth, our spirits dreamed.

Finding Strength in Stitches

With each small stitch, a bond we sew,
In every thread, our courage grows.
The fabric of life, a woven dance,
In trials met, we take a chance.

Through frayed edges, we find our way,
Mending hearts each passing day.
The needles pierce, but do not break,
In healing seams, our souls awake.

From patch to patch, we rise anew,
In unity, our strength shines through.
Together stitched, we shall withstand,
The storms of life, hand in hand.

Embracing the Unseen

In shadows where whispers play,
Dreams intertwine with the night.
Fingers trace the air's soft sway,
Hoping to catch glimpses of light.

Moonlight spills on silent streams,
Echoes dance in the cool breeze.
Unraveled threads of hidden dreams,
Embrace the depths with gentle ease.

Each heartbeat is a secret told,
In the quiet, we learn to see.
Mirrored visions, brave and bold,
Holding close what strives to be.

Through the mist, a path unfolds,
Leading hearts to realms unseen.
With every step, the courage molds,
To seek the truths that lie between.

Spinning the Unknown

In the cradle of a silent night,
Thoughts weave through the fabric of stars.
Each moment whispers bold delight,
Encasing hopes in silver jars.

Winds carry tales from afar,
Spinning dreams on a fragile thread.
Every heartbeat, a guiding star,
Leading souls where none have tread.

Hands that shape the clay of fate,
Molding futures with tender grace.
In the depths where shadows wait,
Awakens joy in this vast space.

As dawn kisses the waking earth,
The unknown dances, wild and free.
In the journey, we find our worth,
Creating life's sweet tapestry.

The Texture of Tomorrow

Morning breaks with soft embrace,
Threads of gold on dewy grass.
The world awakens, finds its place,
In each moment, fleeting, vast.

Colors blend in sky's warm hue,
Woven dreams in azure glow.
Every heartbeat, fresh and new,
Crafting paths where visions flow.

Hands outstretched toward the dawn,
Every moment ripe with chance.
In the fabric, futures drawn,
Life unfolds in a sacred dance.

With each choice, we build and break,
The texture of our endless quest.
In tomorrow's hands, we awake,
To shape what lies within our chest.

Driftwood of Desire

Upon the shore, old stories lie,
Driftwood whispers of the sea.
Each piece carries a soft sigh,
Of dreams that yearn to break free.

Waves kiss the weathered grain,
Salted air speaks of the past.
In the tides, we feel the strain,
Of hopes that anchor, yet outlast.

Through the ebb, through the flow,
Desires rise with the moon's pull.
With every crest, we learn to grow,
As our hearts remain so full.

In the dance of shifting tides,
We find a truth that holds us near.
For every driftwood that abides,
Is a wish, a longing, sincere.

Loom of Serenity

In twilight's hush, the world retreats,
Dreams woven soft, where silence greets.
Colors blend in gentle grace,
A tapestry of time and space.

Peace's fabric, warm and tight,
Stitches of day dance with night.
Each thread whispers tales of old,
In the loom, serenity's fold.

With every pass, a story told,
Of love and loss, of brave and bold.
Within this work, the heart finds home,
In the loom's embrace, no need to roam.

So let us weave, with mindful hands,
The fabric of life, as fate commands.
Each moment captured, rich and free,
In the loom of our shared serenity.

Through the Needle's Eye

A tiny portal, a slender space,
Where dreams arrive and fears erase.
Through the needle, visions flow,
Magic hidden, waiting to show.

A thread of hope pulled from the dark,
Connecting souls with a tiny spark.
In every stitch, a wish takes flight,
Through the needle's eye, we seek the light.

With patient hands, we guide the way,
In life's great fabric, come what may.
Each tension met, each knot undone,
In this dance, we're all as one.

Beyond the hole, a vast expanse,
In every struggle, there lies a chance.
Through the needle's eye, we find our course,
A thread of love, a powerful force.

The Threads We Follow

In the depths of quiet night,
Threads of fate begin their flight.
Twisting paths that intertwine,
Leading us to love's design.

Each color rich, each hue a hold,
Stories from the brave and bold.
Fingers trace what hearts should know,
The threads we follow help us grow.

Through joy and sorrow, loss and gain,
Woven in laughter, stitched in pain.
In every loop, a lesson learned,
With every turn, our passion burned.

So take my hand, let's walk this line,
In every thread, your heart and mine.
Together we weave, together we spin,
In the tapestry, our lives begin.

Knots of Ambition

In shadows cast by dreams above,
We find the knots we weave in love.
Every twist, a challenge faced,
In the heart of ambition, we are chased.

With passion fiery, we take the stage,
Each knot a mark, a story page.
Tangled paths that lead us here,
In pursuit of dreams, we persevere.

The threads may fray, but not our will,
In every setback, we find the thrill.
For in the struggle, strength ignites,
In knots of ambition, we reach new heights.

So tie your dreams and hold them tight,
In the darkest hour, find the light.
With every knot, a chance to soar,
In the weave of ambition, forevermore.

Hidden Stitches of Strength

In shadows where the silence dwells,
The whispers of resilience swell.
Beneath the surface, threads hold tight,
Weaving strength into the night.

Each tiny stitch, a story told,
In tangled fabric, brave and bold.
With every pull, we learn to bend,
From broken seams, we rise again.

Embrace the flaws, let beauty show,
In hidden stitches, courage grows.
With hands that mend and hearts that care,
We find the strength to be laid bare.

So let us cherish each fine line,
For through the cracks, true light will shine.
In every tear, a chance to see,
The hidden strength that sets us free.

The Power of a Tied Knot

Two threads entwined, a sacred bond,
In ties of love, we learn to respond.
With strength they hold, through stormy weather,
Together we can face whatever.

A simple loop, yet strong and tight,
In every struggle, it brings light.
With every twist, a promise made,
In knotted dreams, our fears will fade.

Through trials faced and battles fought,
The threads of life, a lesson taught.
In tangled tales and woven grace,
A knot of hope, we will embrace.

So tie your knots with gentle care,
And know that love is always there.
In every moment, tied and true,
The power of a knot shines through.

Mending Hearts, Stitch by Stitch

With fragile hands, we gently sew,
The hearts that break, the love that grows.
Stitch by stitch, we find our way,
Through tender wounds, light finds its play.

In moments soft, the threads connect,
Lines of hope, we will protect.
Each pull a prayer, each knot a hug,
In mending hearts, we're snug as a bug.

Through layers worn, we learn to heal,
The pain revealed, a chance to feel.
From woven patterns, we reclaim,
A tapestry of love, not shame.

So let us sew with threads divine,
In every heart, a chance to shine.
Mending is art, where love resides,
Stitch by stitch, our spirit guides.

The Pattern of Persistence

In every challenge, a unique design,
The threads of life, they intertwine.
With colors bold, we venture forth,
Creating patterns of our worth.

Through trials faced and lessons learned,
The fires of life have brightly burned.
Each stitch a step, each knot a fight,
In persistence lies our inner light.

As we unravel and reweave dreams,
The fabric changes, or so it seems.
Yet in the chaos, beauty blooms,
In patterns woven from our looms.

So let us step with steady hearts,
And forge a path where courage starts.
With each new thread, we find our place,
The pattern of persistence, we embrace.

Patterns of Perseverance

In the fabric of time, we weave our dreams,
Through trials and tears, hope always beams.
Stitch by stitch, we gather our might,
Creating a tapestry, bold and bright.

With every setback, we stand and rise,
Determined hearts, reaching for the skies.
Each pattern a story, a lesson learned,
In the dance of life, our passion burned.

Through storms and shadows, we find our way,
Guided by stars that refuse to sway.
In the loom of struggle, we craft our fate,
The patterns of perseverance, we celebrate.

So let us embrace the threads that bind,
With courage and strength, our paths aligned.
For in every challenge, a chance to grow,
In the patterns of life, our spirits glow.

Stitching Light from Shadows

In the quiet night, shadows softly fall,
Yet within the dark, we hear the call.
Threads of silver, weaving through the gray,
Stitching together, light finds its way.

Each moment a whisper, hope's gentle sigh,
Transforming the dark as we learn to fly.
With needles of courage, we pierce the night,
In the loom of our hearts, we find the light.

Embracing the shadows, we come alive,
In the depths of despair, we start to thrive.
Stitch by stitch, we mend the seams,
Creating a quilt, sewn from our dreams.

So let us gather, under starry skies,
With laughter and love, where our spirit ties.
For in each shadow, there's a chance to see,
The beauty of light and who we can be.

The Loom of Longing

In the loom of longing, threads intertwine,
With every heartbeat, a tale to divine.
Desires like colors, vivid and bold,
In the tapestry of life, our stories unfold.

With each passing moment, we seek and yearn,
Through dreams and whispers, the fires burn.
Stitching the fragments of what could have been,
In the loom of our souls, new hopes begin.

Fingers weaving memories, rich and deep,
Carving out spaces where secrets sleep.
In the quiet of night, our wishes roam,
In the tapestry of longing, we find our home.

So let us embrace this exquisite thread,
In the dance of desires, let love be spread.
For in every longing, a chance to be,
Closer to the dreams that set our hearts free.

Twisting Doubts into Delights

In the garden of thoughts, doubts bloom and grow,
Yet from the darkness, delights will show.
With gentle hands, we twist and turn,
Transforming the fears, as we patiently learn.

Each worry a seed, planted in fate,
Nurtured with care, we'll cultivate.
Twisting the doubts into threads of gold,
In the harvest of life, new stories unfold.

Through the noise of fear, we find our song,
A melody sweet, where we all belong.
With courage to bend, and strength to invite,
We create a symphony, turning dark into light.

So let us rejoice in this wondrous fight,
For every doubt can become a delight.
Together we'll weave, through the shadows we tread,
In the tapestry of life, let joy be widespread.

Looming Light in Dark Corners

In shadows deep where doubts reside,
A flicker glows, a silent guide.
It dances softly, bold yet shy,
Whispering hope, a gentle sigh.

When fears creep in, and darkness lingers,
The light extends its warmest fingers.
It carves a path through thick despair,
Looming bright, it banishes care.

With every step, it grows more clear,
A beacon bright for all to steer.
In corners dark, where few dare roam,
The looming light will lead us home.

The Warp of Wishes

Within the heart, a wish does weave,
Threads of dreams that we believe.
Each stitch a hope, a vision bright,
The fabric glows in muted light.

A tapestry of desires spun,
In every shade, a tale begun.
With every yearning, futures twist,
Crafting paths that can't be missed.

In gentle curves, the wishes swell,
A pattern blooms, a magic spell.
Through time and space, they intertwine,
The warp of wishes, fate's design.

Unraveling Nightmares into Daydreams

In the stillness before dawn,
Nightmares fade, their power gone.
A gentle hand begins to trace,
The shadows shift, revealing grace.

Unraveled threads of fear and fright,
Turn soft and sweet in morning light.
The dreams awaken, take their flight,
Into a world where all feels right.

Each creeping thought once held so tight,
Transforms to visions pure and bright.
With every breath, new hope redeems,
Unraveling nightmares into dreams.

A Canvas of Courage

With colors bold, the brush does sway,
To paint the fears that fade away.
Every stroke a story told,
A canvas rich, a heart of gold.

In shades of strength, the light breaks through,
A masterpiece, both brave and true.
Each line a testament to fight,
Creating beauty from the night.

With hands unsteady, yet so brave,
We craft a path, our souls to save.
A canvas waits, our hearts engage,
In strokes of courage, we write our page.

Threads of Time and Transformation

In the fabric of life, threads entwine,
Stories of old, both yours and mine.
Each moment a stitch, in colors so bright,
Woven together, they dance in the light.

Seasons shift, and patterns may change,
Yet through the chaos, we learn to arrange.
With every ending, a new start to find,
Embracing the journey, heart and mind combined.

Threadbare memories, still holding tight,
Stitches of laughter, joys taking flight.
Through trials and triumphs, we find our way,
In threads of time, we forever stay.

The loom keeps spinning, turning with grace,
Each strand a lesson, in this sacred space.
Transformation whispers in the silent night,
As we weave our dreams, shining ever bright.

Embracing Imperfection

Flaws like jewels, in shadows they gleam,
Perfectly imperfect, life's honest theme.
Cracks in the surface, tell stories of old,
Of battles once fought, of hearts brave and bold.

In every stumble, a lesson is found,
In the dance of the heart, we're gently unbound.
Embracing the chaos, the flaws we commend,
For it's in our journeys, we beautifully blend.

With every break, we learn how to heal,
To find strength in weakness, and joy in the real.
In the tapestry woven, our stories combine,
We're art made from love, one stitch at a time.

Perfection a myth, in the grand play we see,
It's the quirky and wild that sets us all free.
So here's to the moments, both crooked and bright,
Embracing our truths, we dance in the light.

The Warmth of Woven Wishes

From threads of desire, dreams come alive,
In the loom of our hearts, hopes will survive.
Whispers of longing, in every embrace,
The warmth of our wishes, time cannot erase.

A tapestry stitched with laughter and tears,
Binding together the joys and the fears.
As the patterns evolve, our spirits align,
In the warmth of connection, our souls intertwine.

Each wish a stitch, weaving tales of the heart,
Uniting our spirits, never to part.
In the quiet of night, beneath star-laden skies,
We gather our hopes, as the dawn slowly sighs.

So let us weave magic in bonds of the soul,
With wishes like stars, making the whole.
In the fabric of friendship, and love that persists,
We find the true warmth in woven wishes.

The Looming Horizon of Hope

In the distance, the sun begins to rise,
Painting the world in golden hues and skies.
With every dawn, new dreams take their flight,
On the loom of tomorrow, they shimmer with light.

Bound by the threads of deep-rooted belief,
Each moment a promise, a glimmer, relief.
Through shadows of doubt, we stand side by side,
Chasing our visions, with hope as our guide.

The horizon stretches, vast and profound,
A canvas awaiting, where dreams can be found.
In the fabric of time, we weave our designs,
Unraveling fears, where courage aligns.

So let us reach forth, past struggles and strife,
Embracing the journey, the beauty of life.
With every new day, let our spirits elope,
For on this vast horizon, we'll find our hope.

Transforming Grief into Grace

In shadows deep, sorrow hides,
A heart once broken, it abides.
Yet through the tears, a light appears,
Turning the pain to gentle years.

With whispered hope, a soft embrace,
We learn to move, we learn to trace.
Each tear that falls, a story told,
Transforming grief into pure gold.

Embracing loss, we start to heal,
With every wound, new strength we feel.
A dance of memory, love remains,
In grief's hold still, grace entertains.

So let us rise from sorrow's bed,
With open hearts, we forge ahead.
For in each shadow, there's a spark,
Transforming grief, igniting the dark.

Twine of Tenacity

In tangled roots, we find our ground,
A strength in struggle, life unwound.
With every challenge, we entwine,
The thread of courage, pure and fine.

Through storms we bend, yet do not break,
With hearts unyielding, we undertake.
In weaving dreams, we find our way,
The twine of tenacity holds sway.

Each knot we tie, a lesson learned,
In fire's forge, our spirits burned.
Together, strong, we rise and climb,
In every trial, we dance with time.

United by battles, side by side,
With hope as compass, we will abide.
Through every journey, fate shall see,
The twine of tenacity sets us free.

Crafting Calm from Chaos

In whirlwind days where noise resides,
We seek the peace that softly hides.
Amid the chaos, hearts lay bare,
Crafting calm with mindful care.

With gentle breaths, we find our flow,
In stillness, seeds of patience grow.
A quiet moment, a soothing balm,
Transforming turmoil into calm.

Through raging storms and restless nights,
We gather strength, igniting lights.
With open minds, we forge a way,
Crafting calm from disarray.

The art of balance, ever sought,
In chaos, dreams and hopes are caught.
With every rhythm, we embrace,
A tranquil heart in time and space.

Hues of Happiness and Heartache

In shades of joy, we paint the sky,
Yet in the depths, some shadows lie.
With vibrant strokes, we chase the light,
Hues of happiness, fierce and bright.

But heartache whispers in the breeze,
A reminder woven through the trees.
In every loss, a love remains,
Through all the colors, joy sustains.

We blend the shades, the dark and bright,
Creating beauty through the night.
In life's canvas, we intertwine,
Hues of love and pain align.

With every heartbeat, art unfolds,
A story told, in whispers bold.
For in this tapestry we weave,
Happiness and heartache, we believe.

Golden Threads of Inspiration

Golden threads weave through dreams,
Sparkling in the morning light.
With each stitch, new visions gleam,
Guiding hearts to take their flight.

Whispers of a silent muse,
Inviting thoughts to dance and spin.
From shadows, colors brightly fuse,
Creating worlds we long to win.

In every fold, a story flows,
Of hopes, of wishes, bold and bright.
The fabric of our lives bestows,
A tapestry of pure delight.

Crafted with love, each thread we tie,
Threads of inspiration intertwine.
In this embrace, we learn to fly,
Finding joy in every line.

The Needle of New Beginnings

A needle pierces through the night,
Stitching dreams to morning skies.
In every pull, a chance to write,
A tale of hope that never dies.

Threads of courage, soft yet strong,
Weave a quilt of fresh starts here.
In every place where we belong,
New journeys beckon, bright and clear.

So gather all your fears and doubts,
And place them on the pattern wide.
With every knot, let joy sprout,
Embrace the change, let fear subside.

The needle's touch is gentle, sure,
As new beginnings take their form.
In every seam, a love that's pure,
We find our strength in every storm.

Embracing the Unraveling

In threads that fray, we find our way,
The frictions of a life well-lived.
With every twist, we dare to play,
Accepting all that time has given.

Embracing flaws, we mend and fold,
The beauty in the imperfect art.
In every crease, a truth unfolds,
A patchwork woven with the heart.

Let go of fears that tightly squeeze,
As fabric breathes, we stand unveiled.
In unravelling, our spirits ease,
A newfound strength where love prevailed.

So take a step, let loose control,
In chaos lies the chance to mend.
Embrace the unraveling of the whole,
For in the threads, beginnings blend.

Weft of Whimsy

With whimsy woven through the night,
Colors splash like dreams on air.
In laughter's threads, we find delight,
A playful dance, light as a prayer.

A tapestry of joy unfolds,
Where serendipity takes flight.
The weft of whimsy gently holds,
A world that's bright, pure, and light.

In every stitch, a story's spun,
Of laughter shared beneath the moon.
With every thread, our hearts are won,
Creating magic, night to noon.

So let the colors blend and sway,
Together, weaving dreams so free.
In the fabric of a joyful play,
We find forever's jubilee.

The Unraveled Story

Words whispered softly in the night,
Memories dance in fading light.
Threads of truth, tangled and worn,
In the silence, a new tale is born.

Echoes linger where shadows play,
Each heartbeat marks a fleeting day.
History's weight, both heavy and light,
A puzzle pieced, hidden from sight.

Fingers trace where the ink has dried,
Secrets unveiled, no longer to hide.
Pages turn with a gentle sigh,
In every heartbeat, a reason why.

So let the stories unfold with grace,
In every wrinkle, a tender face.
Unraveled paths lead to the unknown,
In the quiet, true love has grown.

A Knot Tied in Faith

In a world where doubts entwine,
A bond is formed, pure and divine.
With every loop and every twist,
Our hopes emerge from shadowed mist.

Holding tight through storms that rage,
Trust binds us on this sacred page.
In the silence, a promise stays,
Guiding us through life's winding maze.

Each knot a story, each weave a dream,
Together, we flow like a rushing stream.
United we stand, though tides may shift,
Our hearts are strong, a timeless gift.

With faith as our anchor, we rise anew,
Facing the tides with a steadfast view.
In knots of love, we find our way,
Through trials and triumphs, come what may.

Tapestries of Change

Colors blend in a vibrant thread,
Each stitch whispers of tales unsaid.
Time weaves onward with a steady hand,
Crafting futures, brave and grand.

Seasons shift, and patterns break,
In every change, new dreams we make.
Fragile threads may fray or bend,
Yet beauty lingers; it will not end.

Woven histories in every hue,
Fade into stories, old yet new.
In the fabric of lives, we find our place,
A tapestry rich with love and grace.

Change is constant, a dance so bold,
In its embrace, we learn to hold.
Each layer added, a story bright,
Weaving hope in the tapestry of light.

Shadows Shaping Light

In the quiet, shadows twine,
Crafting forms both strong and fine.
Light breaks through in gentle streams,
Illuminating our layered dreams.

In the darkness, we fear no more,
For shadows whisper of the core.
Where light is cast, the shapes grow clear,
Guiding us softly as we draw near.

Every shadow bears a name,
A witness to both loss and gain.
Together they dance, a waltz of fate,
In their embrace, we find our state.

With every sunrise, shadows fade,
Yet in their depths, our truths parade.
Shaping light with every breath,
In dreams remembered, we conquer death.

Patterns of the Heart

In shadows cast by love's embrace,
We weave a dance, a tender trace.
The echoes blend in muted hues,
Each pulse a song, each charm a muse.

In quiet corners, dreams entwine,
The threads of fate in time align.
With every beat, a rhythm flows,
A tapestry of highs and lows.

Through storms that shake the silent night,
Our hearts reveal a fleeting light.
In colors bright, we paint our fears,
The patterns told through laughter, tears.

Together we embrace the art,
Creating solace, heart to heart.
In woven paths, forever roam,
In patterns bold, we find our home.

From Frayed Ends to New Beginnings

A thread once worn, now torn apart,
Yet in its fray, there beats a heart.
With gentle hands, we tie a knot,
From endings lost, new dreams are caught.

In every tear, a story lies,
Of whispered hopes and silent cries.
We stitch together, piece by piece,
From frayed to whole, we find our peace.

The dawn arrives with colors bright,
Each sunrise whispers, take your flight.
From ashes cold, a fire shall gleam,
A journey borne from every dream.

So let us braid the past with grace,
And wander forward, time's embrace.
From frayed ends rise to skies anew,
In every heartbeat, courage grew.

The Quilt of Yearning

In patches rich, our dreams unfold,
Stories woven, tales retold.
Each square a wish, a silent prayer,
In quilted warmth, we linger there.

Through nights of longing, hearts awake,
We trace the seams that love can make.
Every stitch, a finger's touch,
In threads of hope, we feel so much.

With whimsy bright, we dance and sway,
In every fold, a child at play.
The quilt of yearning, soft and wide,
Embraces dreams we cannot hide.

And though the world may pull apart,
Together holds the strongest heart.
In fabric bright, our souls entwine,
The quilt of yearning, ever mine.

Strands of Comfort

In gentle whispers, comfort breathes,
Each strand a promise, heart it weaves.
With every thread, a thought of care,
A silken touch, our worries bare.

Through tangled paths, we find our way,
In fibers strong, we choose to stay.
With hands held tight, we face the night,
As strands of comfort hold us right.

In laughter shared and tears we wipe,
A bond is forged, a world so ripe.
Each fiber tells a tale of grace,
In every hug, we find our place.

So let us gather, close and near,
In strands of comfort, love is clear.
Together, woven, we shall be,
In every heart, a tapestry.

Threads of Hope

In the quiet dawn, a soft embrace,
Whispers of courage in every space,
A fragile thread, yet strong and bright,
Holds the promise of a new flight.

Through the storms that dark clouds cast,
We weave our dreams, hold on steadfast,
Each stitch a story, each knot a prayer,
Binding us close, a bond so rare.

In the tapestry of our shared days,
We find our strength in countless ways,
Embracing light, chasing despair,
A rich design, a life laid bare.

Together we rise, hand in hand,
In the fabric of hope, we firmly stand,
With threads entwined, our hearts ignite,
A woven journey into the light.

Tapestry of Dreams

In twilight's glow, our visions entwine,
Colors so vivid, like stars that shine,
Each thread a wish, a silent song,
A tapestry woven where we belong.

With every heartbeat, dreams take flight,
Crafted by day, embraced by night,
Patterns emerging, as hearts unfold,
Stories of courage and dreams retold.

Through the looms of time, we weave our fate,
Patience and passion, both resonate,
In the dance of fibers, hope finds a way,
A vibrant manifesto of a brighter day.

When shadows loom and doubts invade,
We anchor our hearts, the fabric laid,
Together we stitch, a seamless seam,
In our tapestry of dreams, we dare to dream.

Stitching Shadows to Light

In the depths of night, shadows creep,
Whispers of doubt that make us weep,
Yet through the darkness, a glimmer leads,
With every stitch, we tackle our needs.

Gather the threads of fears we hold,
Knit them tightly, let stories unfold,
In the fabric of struggle, a pattern appears,
A journey of growth, through laughter and tears.

With needles of courage, we pierce the dim,
Transforming the silence, the words feel brim,
Each moment a stitch, binding us tight,
Turning the shadows into radiant light.

Together we rise, from dark to shine,
Stitching our truths, your heart next to mine,
In the quilt of existence, so rich and bright,
We're stitching shadows, embracing the light.

Fabric of Desires

In the fabric of desires, woven with care,
Threads of passion dancing in the air,
Each wish a fiber, each hope a hue,
Crafting a canvas of dreams anew.

Through the looms of longing, we stitch with grace,
The patterns of life, in a sweet embrace,
In the seams of our hearts, aspirations grow,
As we navigate paths that only we know.

With every heartbeat, our wishes align,
In the tapestry woven, our souls intertwine,
Filling the spaces with warmth and delight,
Creating a masterpiece, bold and bright.

So let us embrace the desires we share,
In the fabric of life, we fashion with care,
For in every thread, love's story sings,
An eternal design of what dreaming brings.

Milton Keynes UK
Ingram Content Group UK Ltd.
UKHW020048251124
451398UK00007BA/235

9 789916 901700